# Fluffy, Flat, and Wet

## A Book About Clouds

by Dana Meachen Rau   illustrated by Denise Shea

PICTURE WINDOW BOOKS
Minneapolis, Minnesota

Thanks to our advisers for their expertise, research, and advice:

Dr. Stanley P. Jones, Assistant Director
NASA-sponsored Classroom of the Future Program

Susan Kesselring, M.A., Literacy Educator
Rosemount–Apple Valley–Eagan (Minnesota) School District

Editorial Director: Carol Jones
Managing Editor: Catherine Neitge
Creative Director: Keith Griffin
Editor: Christianne Jones
Story Consultant: Terry Flaherty
Designer: Joe Anderson
Page Production: Picture Window Books
The illustrations in this book were created digitally.

Picture Window Books
5115 Excelsior Boulevard
Suite 232
Minneapolis, MN 55416
877-845-8392
www.picturewindowbooks.com

Printed in the United States of America.

Library of Congress Cataloging-in-Publication Data
Rau, Dana Meachen, 1971-
Fluffy, flat, and wet : a book about clouds / by Dana Meachen Rau ;
illustrated by Denise Shea.
p. cm. — (Amazing science)
Includes bibliographical references and index.
ISBN 1-4048-1134-6 (hardcover)
1. Clouds—Juvenile literature. 2. Weather—Juvenile literature. I. Shea,
Denise, ill. II. Title. III. Series.

QC921.35.R38 2006
551.57'6—dc22                                          2005003725

# Table of Contents

# Water in the Sky

You drink a glass of water. Your friend sips hot chocolate. The water in your glass is a liquid, and the ice cubes are solids. The steam rising from the hot chocolate is a gas. Liquid, solid, and gas are the three forms of water.

Clouds are made of water. Tiny water droplets and tiny ice pieces collect to form clouds.

**FUN FACT**

Ice, snow, and hail are examples of water as a solid. Steam from a teapot is a gas. Water as a liquid is everywhere, from oceans to your bathtub.

**FUN FACT**
Why don't the droplets in a cloud fall
to the ground? The droplets of water
and ice are so small and so light that
the air can hold them up.

6

## Forming a Cloud

Clouds form when the air is filled with water. When the wet air is warmed by the sun, it rises into the sky like a bubble. This bubble of air cools as it rises. The water in the air turns from a gas into a liquid or a solid. This process makes a cloud.

# Cirrus and Stratus Clouds

Look up in the sky. You may notice that not all clouds look alike. There are different types of clouds.

Cirrus clouds are very high in the sky. They are made of ice. They look like wisps of hair, horse tails, or feathers.

Stratus clouds are low and made of water. They cover the sky like a huge gray blanket.

**FUN FACT**
Fog is stratus clouds resting very close to the ground.

# Cumulus and Nimbus Clouds

The sky may be filled with clouds that look like scoops of ice cream or puffs of cotton candy. These clouds are cumulus clouds.

Sometimes puffy clouds are dark gray instead of white. These clouds usually bring rain. They are called nimbus clouds.

## FUN FACT

People can look at clouds and use them to predict, or figure out, what the weather will be.

**FUN FACT**

The water droplets in a cloud are very small. It takes about 100 of these tiny droplets to make one raindrop.

# The Sky Is Falling!

Do you hide under an umbrella on a rainy day? Do you like to splash in puddles?

Droplets in a cloud join together to make a raindrop. When the raindrop gets large and heavy, it falls out of the cloud. It's raining!

**FUN FACT**

No two snowflakes are alike. They all have one thing in common, though. They all have six sides.

# Frozen Water

When clouds become very cold, the water in the cloud freezes into small pieces of ice. These pieces of ice join together to form snowflakes. The snowflakes fall to the ground. If enough snowflakes fall, you may have enough to make a snowman!

# Stormy Weather

From the ground, clouds look quiet and still. But it is busy inside a cloud. Strong winds blow. Sometimes, the winds make droplets in a cloud rub or crash against each other. This movement makes a spark that shoots out of the cloud. This spark is called lightning.

## FUN FACT

Have you ever walked across a carpet in your socks and then touched a doorknob? You might make a spark. Clouds make sparks, too. In a cloud, the rubbing raindrops make a spark we call lightning.

## The Stormiest Clouds

Tornadoes are some of the stormiest clouds. A tornado is a funnel-shaped cloud that touches the ground. It twirls and spins with strong winds. When tornadoes are around, you should go to a basement or an inside room to stay safe.

**FUN FACT**

There are usually warning signs that a tornado is coming. The sky often turns a greenish color, clouds move very fast, and a loud roaring sound fills the air.

**FUN FACT**

Clouds are not always white or gray. When the sun is rising or setting, its light bounces off the clouds and can make them orange, pink, blue, and purple.

## Changing Pictures

Clouds are always changing. Winds might blow them across the sky. Their water might dry up on a sunny day. They might drop all of their water as rain until they disappear.

Look up at the sky. Does that cloud look like a castle? Does it look like a comfy pillow? Does it look like a fire-breathing dragon? Clouds can look like anything you imagine.

# Keep a Cloud Journal

**What you need:**

- ✳ a notebook of unlined paper
- ✳ a pencil
- ✳ an outdoor thermometer

**What you do:**

1. On the first page of your notebook, write the date.

2. Check the thermometer to see the temperature of the air, and write it down.

3. Write down what the weather is like. Is the sky clear? Is the sky gray? Is it raining, snowing, or sunny?

4. Draw a picture of the clouds you see. Do they look like popcorn? Do they look like ripples of sand?

5. Go out every day at about the same time. Each day, use a new page of your notebook to write the date and temperature and make a cloud drawing.

6. After a month, look back through your notebook. What types of clouds were out on rainy days or sunny days? What types were out on warm days or cold days?

7. Now that you've kept a cloud journal, can you look at the clouds in the sky and guess what the weather might be?

# Cloud Facts

### Lots of Clouds
There are other types of clouds besides cirrus, stratus, cumulus, and nimbus. All types of clouds have names based on their shape and how high they are in the sky.

### Caps and Pancakes
Land can affect the shapes of the clouds that form over it. Cap clouds often sit on the tops of mountains. Clouds that look like stacks of pancakes form over rough, flat land.

### High-up Views
We watch clouds from beneath. People in airplanes, however, are able to look down on clouds if they fly high enough. Astronauts get the highest view of all when they are in spaceships orbiting Earth.

### Other Planets
The reason we have clouds on Earth is because our planet has water. No other planet in our solar system is known to have water, yet many have clouds. Clouds on other planets are made of gases. These gases make clouds that are blue, orange, or brown.

### The Force of Friction
When two objects rub together, they make friction. When rain droplets in a cloud rub together, they make friction. This friction makes the electric spark we call lightning.

# Glossary

friction—the rubbing of one surface against another
lightning—the electricity caused by friction in a cloud
liquid—a substance that can be poured
predict—to figure out what may happen in the future
solid—a substance that has shape
tornadoes—a windstorm with a funnel-shaped cloud that touches the ground

# To Learn More

## At the Library

Bauer, Marion Dane. *Clouds*. New York: Aladdin, 2004.

Eubank, Mark E. *The Weather Detectives: Fun Filled Facts, Experiments, and Activities for Kids*. Gibbs Smith Publishers, 2004.

Sherman, Josepha. *Shapes in the Sky*. Minneapolis: Picture Window Books, 2004.

## On the Web

FactHound offers a safe, fun way to find Web sites related to this book. All of the sites on FactHound have been researched by our staff. *www.facthound.com*

1. Visit the FactHound home page.
2. Enter a search word related to this book, or type in this special code: 1404811346
3. Click on the FETCH IT button.

Your trusty FactHound will fetch the best Web sites for you!

## Look for all of the books in the Amazing Science: Exploring the Sky series:

**Fluffy, Flat, and Wet:** A Book About Clouds
**Hot and Bright:** A Book About the Sun
**Night Light:** A Book About the Moon
**Space Leftovers:** A Book About Comets, Asteroids, and Meteoroids
**Spinning in Space:** A Book About the Planets
**Spots of Light:** A Book About Stars